PIANO
VOCAL

contemporary
cabaret

ISBN 0-7935-7674-1

HAL•LEONARD®
CORPORATION
7777 W. BLUEMOUND RD. P.O. BOX 13819 MILWAUKEE, WI 53213

INDEXED

Visit Hal Leonard Online at
www.halleonard.com

And I'll Be There

Words by ALAN and MARILYN BERGMAN
Music by DAVE GRUSIN

I'll be there with you _____ when - ev - er _____
shad - ows come _____ and moon - light _____
times when friends _____ de - sert you _____

the world seems far too wide. _____
paints pic - tures on the wall, _____
and life may let you down. _____

Blizzard of Lies

Words and Music by DAVE FRISHBERG
and SAMANTHA FRISHBERG

We must have lunch real soon, your
You may have won a prize, your won't
We'll send some-one right out, now

lug - gage is checked through, we've
wrin - kle, shrink, or peel, your
this won't hurt a bit, he's

Butter

Words and Music by
MEGON McDONOUGH

Calling You

Words and Music by
BOB TELSON

Hauntingly

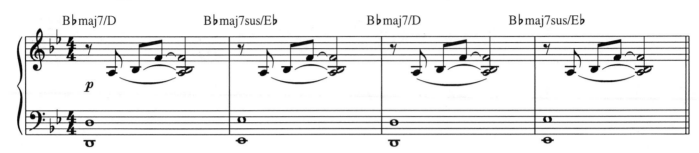

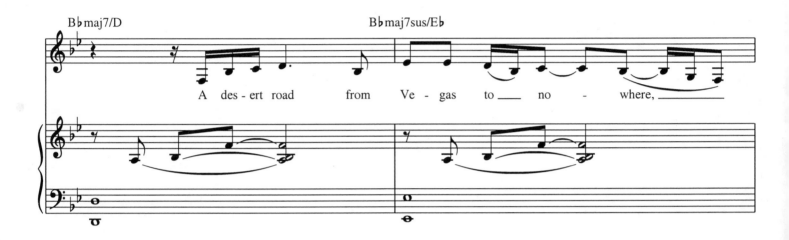

A des-ert road from Ve-gas to ___ no - where, ___

some-place bet - ter ___ than _ where you've been. _

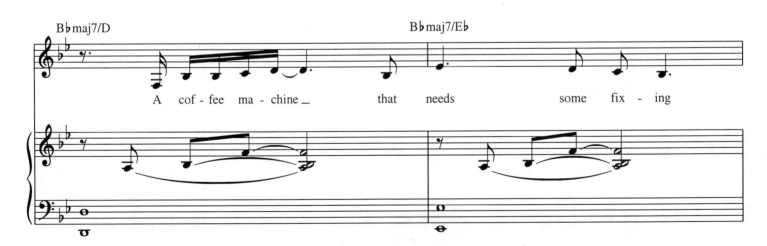

A cof-fee ma-chine _ that needs some fix - ing

Coffee
(In a Cardboard Cup)

Words and Music by FRED EBB
and JOHN KANDER

The trou - ble _ with the world to - day it seems to me _ is
trou - ble _ with the hel - ter skel - ter life we lead _ is

cof - fee in a card - board cup.
cof - fee in a card - board cup.

The
The

trou - ble _ with the af - flu - ent so - ci - e - ty _ is
trou - ble _ the psy - cho - lo - gists have all a - greed _ is

Good Thing He Can't Read My Mind

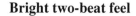

Words and Music by
CHRISTINE LAVIN

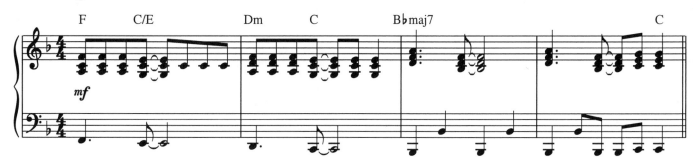

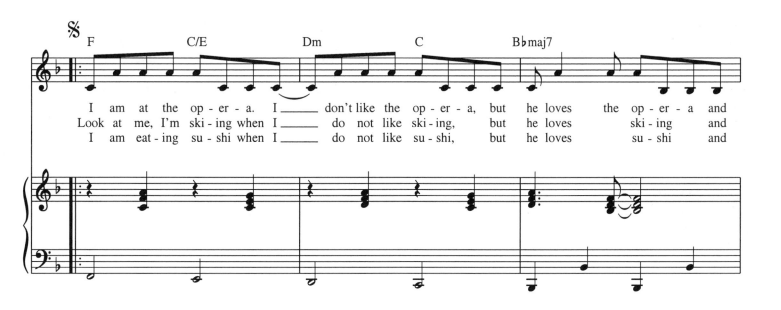

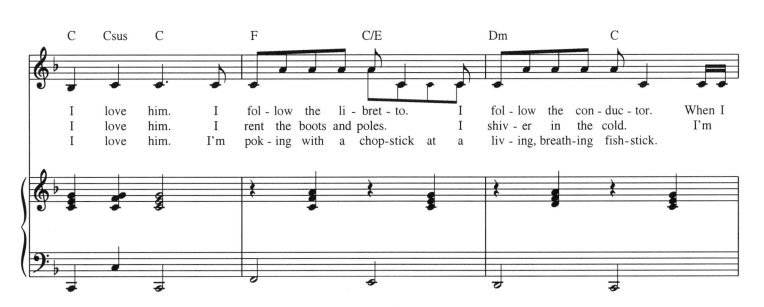

I am at the op - er - a. I _____ don't like the op - er - a, but he loves the op - er - a and
Look at me, I'm ski - ing when I _____ do not like ski - ing, but he loves ski - ing and
I am eat - ing su - shi when I _____ do not like su - shi, but he loves su - shi and

I love him. I fol - low the li - bret - to. I fol - low the con - duc - tor. When I
I love him. I rent the boots and poles. I shiv - er in the cold. I'm
I love him. I'm pok - ing with a chop - stick at a liv - ing, breath - ing fish - stick.

D.S. al Coda
(take 2nd ending)

'cause he's a smok-er. I'm play-ing chess, though I con-fess, some-times I long for pok - er.

CODA

So if you see me in a su - shi bar,

see me on the mez - za - nine, see me on a ski slope look - ing scared,

hey, don't feel sor - ry for me. I must be in love. Oh, why in the hell __ else would

Flight

Music and Lyric by
CRAIG CARNELIA

Delicately ($\quarternote$ = 112)

mp espres.

Ped.

Ped. sim. throughout

Let me run thru a field in the night, let me lift from the ground 'til my

soul is in flight. Let me sway like the shade of a tree, let me

(*) - Play both the written note and the note an octave lower.

* "Ay" sound flows directly from "Ah" sound and is pronounced "Ay" as in "way".

Ah _____

Let me leave be - hind _____ all the clouds ___ in my

mind. ___ I _____ wan-na wake with-out won-der-ing why, ___

He's Not Home Yet

Lyric by BRIAN GARI
Music by DAVID SHIRE

Home Is Where the Heart Is

Words and Music by
SALLY FINGERETT

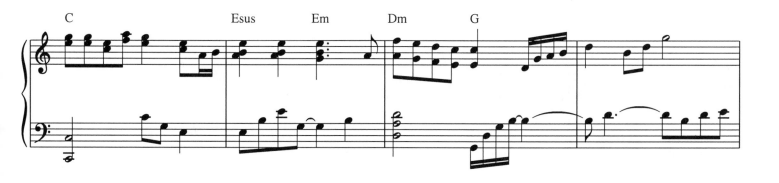

On our cor - ner there's this nice __ man. His name is Mark. He's
Through the yard __ live Deb and Tri - cia with their drills and lad - ders
sits and waits __ with his win-dow o - pen. His house is emp - ty. His

at home. 'Round the cor - ner, here comes Mar - tin. He's a - lone now. He ___ tries smil - ing. ___ He roams a - round ___ his well-stocked kitch - en knows that fate will soon be ___ com -

side your heart where love is, _____ that's where you've got to make your - self _

D.S. al Coda

at home. Mar - tin

CODA

at home. That's where you've got to make your - self _

at home.

rit.

A Horse with Wings

Music and Lyric by
RICKY IAN GORDON

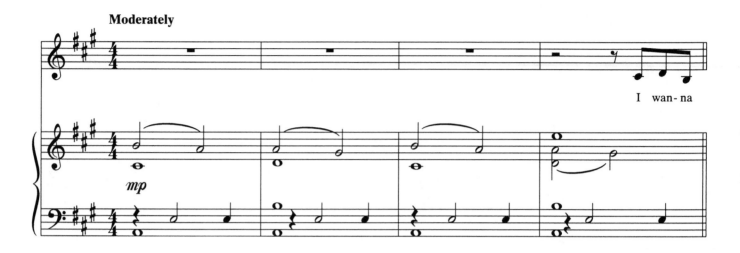

I wan - na cry.
I wan - na

pray that all my wish - es would come true af - ter to - day.
And should I

put a word for you in, should I say an ex - tra Kyr - i - e.

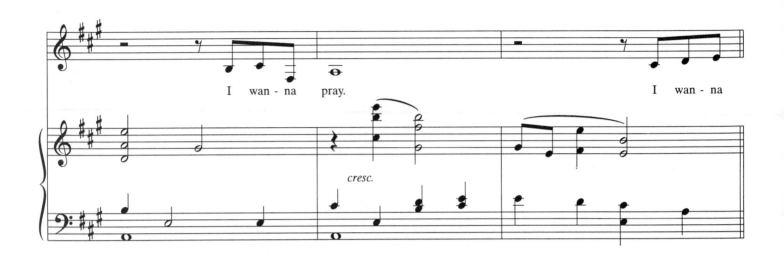

I wan - na pray.   I wan - na

lie,   I wan - na   think that things are bet - ter than they   are.   I wan - na

think we've got - ten fur - ther and that   far   is just an   inch a - way.

I wan-na lie. A horse with wings, I wan-na think of things like that and oth-er things. I want two broth-ers, one who laughs and one who sings. I hope the fu-ture brings a horse with wings. I wan-na

know the things they told me way back when were real - ly so. I wan-na

make a lit - tle mark be - fore I go, not bare - ly just get by.

I wan - na fly.

The Kind of Love You
Never Recover From

Words and Music by
CHRISTINE LAVIN

She has-n't seen him in thir - ty years. _ The men-tion of his name does-n't
But there's a wom-an he still dreams a - bout, _ cer - tain things he's learned to
Years from now will we curse the day _ you let me let you

bring on tears. _ If you ask _ her, "Are there an - y re - grets?" _ she'll tell you
live with - out. _ If you ask _ him, "Are there an - y re - grets?" _ he'll tell you
walk a - way? _ Is - n't this too dear a price to pay _ for the

2nd Verse-omit these measures

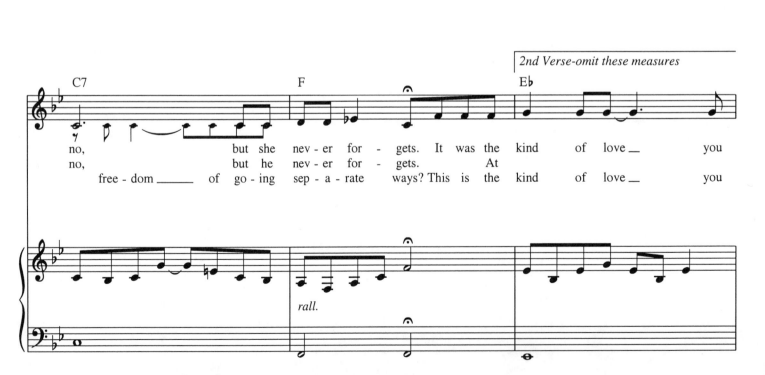

no, but she nev - er for - gets. It was the kind of love _ you
no, but he nev - er for - gets. At
free - dom _ of go - ing sep - a - rate ways? This is the kind of love _ you

rall.

never re-cov-er from, __ e-ven though she found _____ an-oth-er one to take _

never re-cov-er from. __ Don't tell me that I'm gon-na find an-oth - er one to

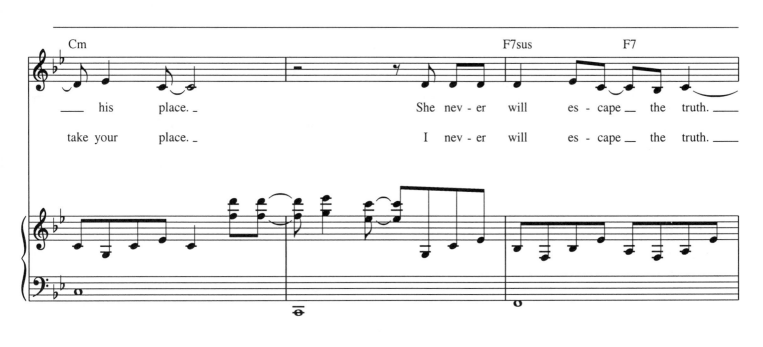

__ his place. _ She nev-er will es-cape __ the truth. ____

take your place. _ I nev-er will es-cape __ the truth. ____

__ At times like this when the moon is right, when the

times like this when the moon is right, when the

__ At times like this when the moon is right, when the

To Coda ⊕

I've Been Taught by Experts

Words and Music by PETER ALLEN
and HAL HACKADY

Lyrics:

I've been taught by ex-perts __ in the art of cru-el-ty. __ Now I'm
bod-y is a bat-tle-field; I've got the scars to show. __ One for

giv-ing __ les-sons free. All it takes is three. I'll
ev-'ry __ yes and no, ev-'ry yes and no. Yes,

It Feels Like Home

Words and Music by
JOHN BUCCHINO

But since we're in this to-geth - er, ___ it feels like ___ home. ___

The Lady Down the Hall

Words and Music by
ANNIE DINERMAN

Living in the Shadows

from VICTOR/VICTORIA

Words by LESLIE BRICUSSE
Music by FRANK WILDHORN

Moderately slow

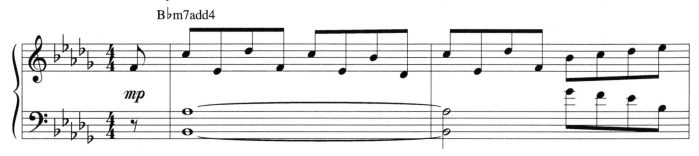

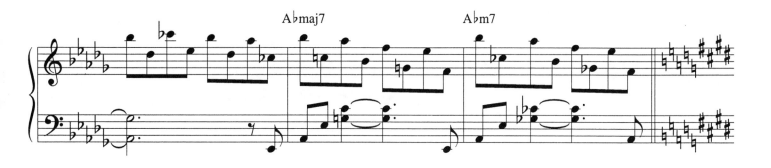

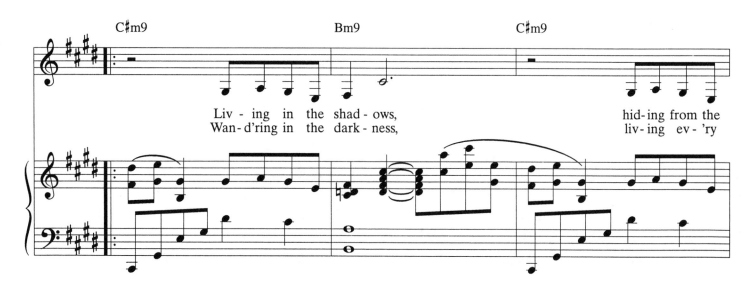

Liv - ing in the shad - ows,
Wan - d'ring in the dark - ness,

hid - ing from the
liv - ing ev - 'ry

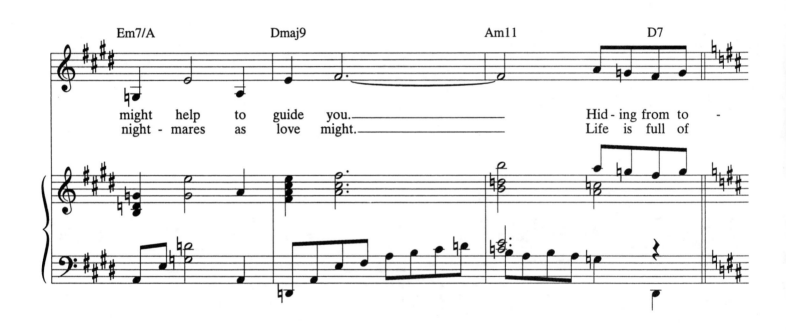

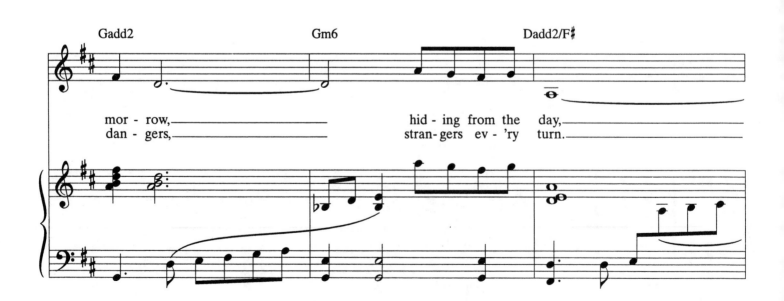

Last One Picked

from Howard Crabtree's WHOOP DEE DOO!

Music by DICK GALLAGHER
Lyrics by MARK WALDROP

TEACHER: "All right, captains, choose your teams!"

* Use your own name.

Laughing Matters

from Howard Crabtree's WHEN PIGS FLY

Music by DICK GALLAGHER
Lyrics by MARK WALDROP

Jay: Live At Five and C N N keep us all a-breast of

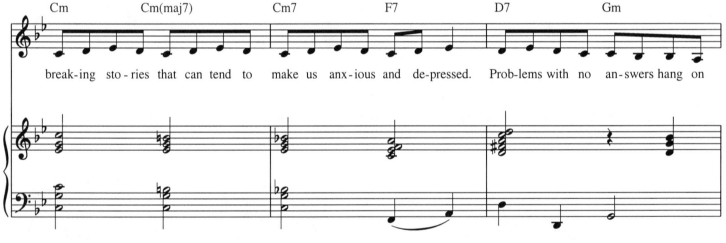

break-ing sto-ries that can tend to make us anx-ious and de-pressed. Prob-lems with no an-swers hang on

like some nag-ging cough, and ev-'ry day some brand new "is-sue" rears its head to piss you off.

Slowly

Bad guys win, __ op - ti - mis - m's wear-ing thin. Things are spin-ning out of con -
Time-bombs tick, __ peo - ple keep on get - ting sick, and a nick-el's not worth a

trol. Cyn - i - cis - m's all the fad. World e - vents could make us mad as
cent. Wick - ed - ness and greed a - bound; just as peace is gain - ing ground it

hat - ters. Al - most ev - 'ry day some un - der - pin - ning slips a - way.
shat - ters. Hate is here to stay, and jus - tice goes to those who pay.

These aren't laugh - ing mat - ters. These aren't laugh - ing

The Next Thing You Know

Words and Music by
CHARLES DeFOREST

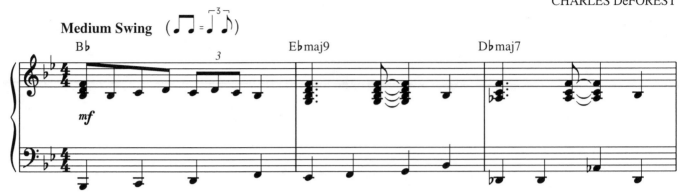

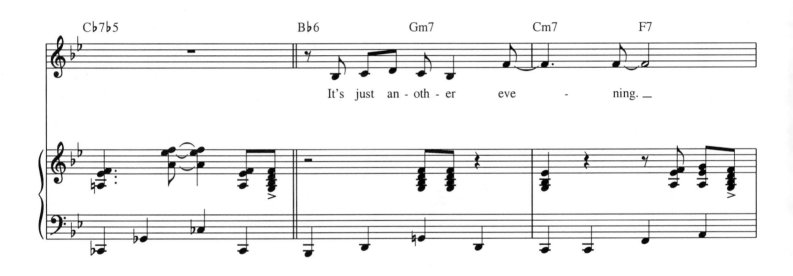

It's just an-oth-er eve - ning. —

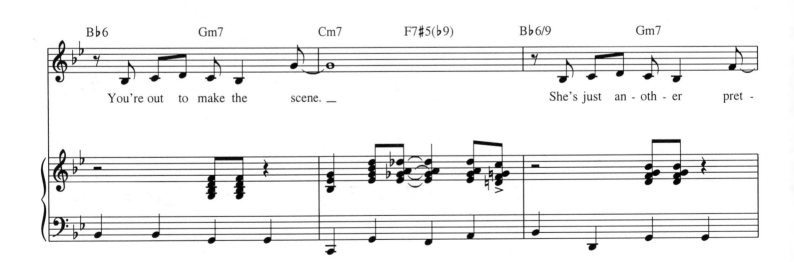

You're out to make the scene. — She's just an-oth-er pret-

Night, Make My Day

from the American Music Theater Festival Production CASINO PARADISE

Words by ARNOLD WEINSTEIN
Music by WILLIAM BOLCOM

* Commissioned by AMTF, which produced the World Premiere, April 7, 1990.

Nothing Like You've Ever Known

from SONG & DANCE

Music by ANDREW LLOYD WEBBER
Lyrics by DON BLACK

Old Movies

Music and Lyric by
CRAIG CARNELIA

In - grid Berg - man flies a - way.

He was friend to no man,

cold - er than a snow - man, but he turns

out A - O - kay.

*Lower notes are optional female melody

(* Lower notes optional female melody)

(* Lower notes optional female melody)

Broader than Tempo I

Tempo I

8va bassa

Once Upon a Dream

from JEKYLL & HYDE

Words by LESLIE BRICUSSE
Music by FRANK WILDHORN

Pearl's a Singer

from SMOKEY JOE'S CAFE

Words and Music by JERRY LEIBER, MIKE STOLLER,
RALPH DINO and JOHN SEMBELLO

Sara Lee

Words by FRED EBB
Music by JOHN KANDER

Sooner or Later
(I Always Get My Man)
from the Film DICK TRACY

Words and Music by
STEPHEN SONDHEIM

Stuck on You
from Howard Crabtree's WHOOP DEE DOO!

Music by DICK GALLAGHER
Lyrics by MARK WALDROP

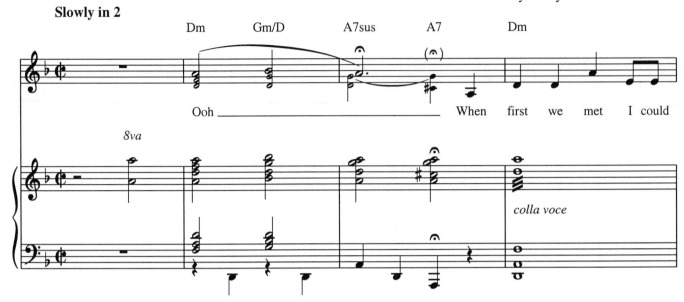

Ooh ___ When first we met I could

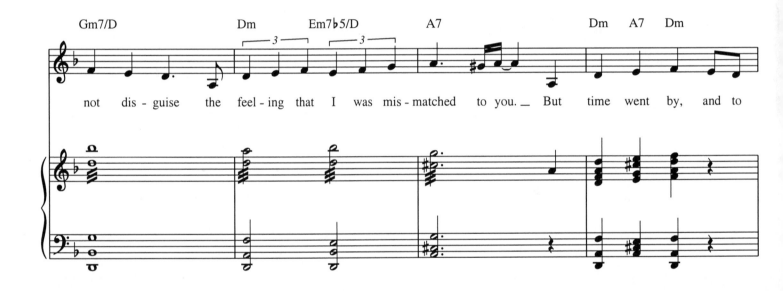

not dis-guise the feel-ing that I was mis-matched to you. _ But time went by, and to

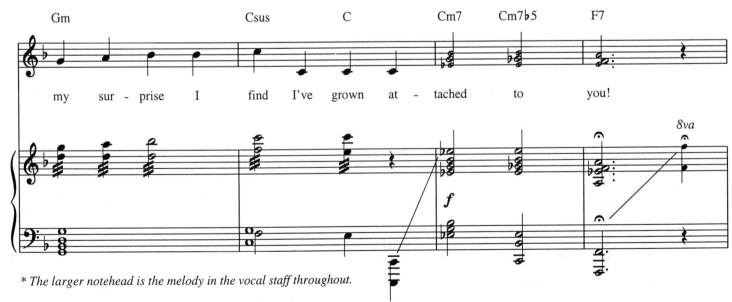

my sur-prise I find I've grown at-tached to you!

* The larger notehead is the melody in the vocal staff throughout.

Fast 30's Swing

Frank - en - stein. _ Ba - by I'm stuck on you. Though I'll ad - mit my

past is check - ered, now my heart is true, ___ like a need - le on a

brok - en re - cord, it's stuck on "I love you" "I love you" "I love you"

"I love you" I'm stuck on you ___ like a gi - ant

Sweet Dreams

Words and Music by
JOHN BUCCHINO

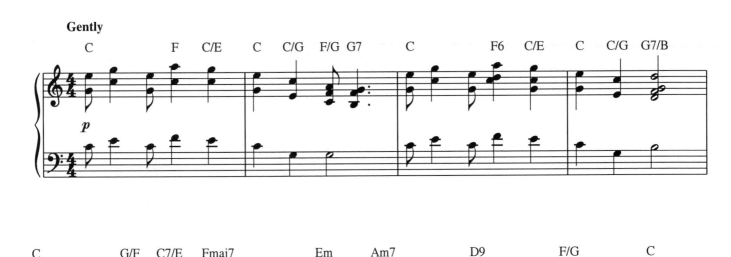

He left a man in New York Cit-y, ___ she broke a home in New Or-leans. ___ They made their way to Cal-i-for-nia.

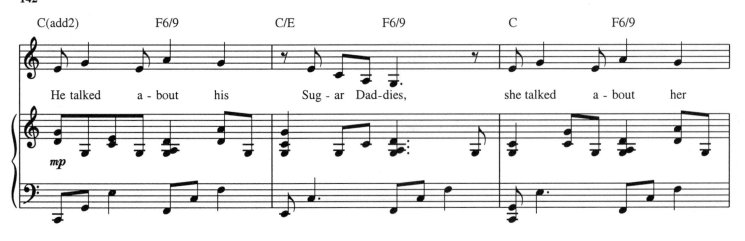

He talked a - bout his Sug - ar Dad-dies, she talked a - bout her

mean ma - rine. ___ They set - tled down ___ in seats ad - join - ing, shar - ing

sweet dreams, ___ sweet dreams. ___

Well, there's no man to sell your heart to ___ when you're

Time Enough for Love

Words and Music by
JIMMY WEBB

When Do the Bells Ring for Me?

Words and Music by
CHARLES DeFOREST

Try with Me

Words and Music by
CHARLES DeFOREST

ways of love, and each ten - der phase of love. Come

face the cold with me and grow old with me._____ I'll be

opt. piano interlude 2nd time, playing melody

all for you and ver - y true, as long as you are sold on me. { And
                                                                          { Re -

if one day { you can - not stay, then soft - ly say good - bye to me. But
mem - ber if {

Without You

from RENT

Words and Music by
JONATHAN LARSON